Managing Editor
Mara Ellen Guckian

Editor in Chief
Karen J. Goldfluss, M.S. Ed.

Creative Director
Sarah M. Smith

Cover Artist
Barb Lorseyedi

Illustrator
Kelly McMahon

Art Coordinator
Renée Mc Elwee

Imaging
James Edward Grace
Craig Gunnell
Amanda R. Harter

Publisher
Mary D. Smith, M.S. Ed.

TCR 3988

**Healthy [...]
for Healthy Kids**

Nutrition & Fitness Activities

CORRELATED TO
National Health Education Standards

✓ Investigate the 5 food groups and examine healthier food options.

✓ Incorporate physical fitness activities into a daily routine.

✓ Make decisions that promote a healthier, happier lifestyle.

Teacher Created Resources

Author
Tracie Heskett, M.Ed.

Teacher Created Resources
12621 Western Avenue
Garden Grove, CA 92841
www.teachercreated.com

ISBN: 978-1-4206-3988-9

©2014 Teacher Created Resources
Reprinted, 2021
Made in U.S.A.

Teacher Created Resources

Table of Contents

Introduction. 3
How to Use This Book 3
Internet Resources. 5
National Health Education Standards. 6
Common Core State Standards. 7
Take the Pledge. 8
Introducing the 5 Food Groups. 9
Exercise of the Day. 11
"Exercise of the Day" Cards. 12

Healthy Foods

Fruits
Fruits Checklist 1 14
Fruits Checklist 2 15
What Is a Fruit?. 16
Fruits That Grow on Trees 17
Fruits That Grow on Vines 18
Citrus Fruits 19
A Rising Star. 20
Favorite Fruits. 21
Which Juice Is Our Favorite? 22

Vegetables
Vegetables Checklist 1 23
Vegetables Checklist 2 24
Vegetables. 25
Our Favorite Vegetables 26
Green Vegetables 27
Hidden Green Beans 28
Peppers 29
Colorful Vegetables 30

Whole Grains
Whole Grains Checklist 31
Whole Grains 32
Whole Wheat Tic-Tac-Toe 33
Oats. 34
Corn. 35
Whole Grain Foods. 36

Dairy Foods
Dairy Foods Checklist. 37
Dairy Foods. 38
Where Milk Comes From 39
Say Cheese 40
Dairy or Not? 41
Dairy Foods for Every Meal 42

Protein Foods
Proteins Foods Checklist. 43
Protein Foods 44
Animals Give Us Protein 45
Legumes 46
Peanuts Are Legumes 47
Nuts We Eat 48
Tree Nuts. 49

Healthy Foods Review
Good Nutrition Is Important 50
"Sometimes" Foods 51
Riddle Time 52
Making Good Food Choices 53
Find the Healthy Foods 54
Hidden Message 55

Healthy Habits
Keeping Our Food Safe 56
Things We Do to Stay Healthy 57
Wash Your Hands. 58
Take Care of Yourself. 59
Healthy Teeth 60
Inside a Tooth 61
Sleep Is Good for Us. 62
Stay Safe 63
Stranger Danger 64
Bones Need Calcium. 65
Being Active 66
Did You Stretch Today? 67
Daily Movements 68
Playing with Movement 69
Animal Moves. 70
Simon Says 71
Ideas for Outdoors. 72
Outdoor Activities Using Props 73
Human Obstacle Course 75
Catch, Throw, and Kick 76
Fitness Fun 77
Baseball. 79
Swimming. 80
Staying Active. 81
Fitness Challenge 82
Food and Fitness Journal. 83
Answer Key 94

Introduction

The *Healthy Habits for Healthy Kids* series was created to provide educators and parents with simple activities that help students learn to make healthy food choices, appreciate the importance of daily exercise, and develop healthy habits they will maintain throughout their lifetimes. Students who are healthy are better able to learn and be successful.

The activities in this book help students understand where the foods they eat come from and why nutritious food choices are beneficial to them. The objectives outlined by the USDA Food Guidance System (*ChooseMyPlate.gov*) formed the foundation upon which the activities in this book are based. Each of the five food groups is explored in depth. The goal is to build an understanding of the need to incorporate fruits, vegetables, whole grains, protein, and dairy into our daily diet. Students will also explore "sometimes" foods, or treats, and develop a greater understanding of why enjoying those foods in moderation is important to their health.

Physical fitness is also of the utmost importance for growing children, and it is suggested that they get at least 60 minutes per day of moderate to vigorous activity. At school and at home this can be difficult, since there is always so much to do. Still, knowing how important physical fitness is, we have to try! We have provided a variety of effective suggestions for exercises that can be done in the classroom. They can be completed in short increments on a daily basis. In addition to the obvious benefits of physical activity, the inclusion of purposeful physical activity at strategic times of the day can release tension and energize both students and teacher.

In recent years, the Common Core State Standards have been developed and are being implemented in many schools. These standards aim to prepare students for college and careers, with an emphasis on real-life applications. Coupled with the National Health Education Standards, they support a whole-child approach to education—one that ensures that each student is healthy, safe, engaged, supported, and challenged in his or her learning. The *Healthy Habits for Healthy Kids* series was developed to support this initiative.

How to Use This Book

Healthy Habits for Healthy Kids was developed to provide busy teachers and students with an easy-to-use curriculum to learn more about personal nutrition, health, and fitness. We want students to embrace making healthy food choices and getting exercise every day, knowing that healthier students make better learners.

Getting Started

- Share the Healthy Habits Pledge (page 8) with students and discuss each line. Challenge students to learn the pledge and share it with family members. The goal here is to inspire the whole family to focus on good nutrition and support healthy habits. Post the pledge in the classroom and review it from time to time as students gain more insights into their personal health.

- Introduce daily exercise to your students using the tips on page 11. On pages 12–13 you will find cards for simple movements that students can do for a minute or two during the day. Display a clock with a second hand or keep a timer handy for these sessions. Use the physical activities to start the day and/or to transition from one activity to another. Throw in an extra one on tough days, or use more than one when weather conditions inhibit outdoor activity. These short, physical exercise breaks are a positive way to settle students for their day's work. And don't forget breathing exercises! They can be done at any time of day and can help refocus or calm students as needed.

Introduction *(cont.)*

How to Use This Book *(cont.)*

Getting Started *(cont.)*

- Gather and display reference materials for the classroom on topics of nutrition, fitness, and overall health. Resources might include library or trade books, magazines, posters, and kid-friendly materials printed from government websites (See page 5.) If appropriate, save links to relevant websites in a dedicated folder on classroom computers.

- Encourage students to start collecting packaging and nutritional labels from food products. Explain that they will be learning to read them and using them for comparisons. Establish an area in the classroom where these can be stored or displayed.

The Student Pages

Student pages present health-related information and activities. Discuss the information together as a class. Share information. Most activities require no more than writing implements and classroom research materials. Devote a certain amount of time each day or week to these activities. The more regular they are, the more important they will be for students.

You might consider interspersing the Healthy Foods activities with Healthy Habits activities to give students a balanced approach. As the teacher, you know how much information your students can absorb at a time. It is also important to be sensitive to the dietary needs and family eating habits of your students.

There are three sections to this book. The first section, Healthy Foods, focuses on the five food groups as described in government materials such as ChooseMyPlate.gov. The goal here is to educate students about healthy foods—what they look like, where they come from, what nutrients they provide, and how they can be incorporated into one's diet. A list of the foods in each food group is found at the beginning of each section. Have students think about the foods they eat regularly, the foods they have not heard of, and healthy foods they would like to try. Provide resource materials for students to learn about foods that are new to them. Encourage students to make healthy food choices each day.

In the Healthy Habits section, students are introduced to concepts such as food safety, germ prevention, dental care, physical fitness, and other ways to stay safe and healthy.

Suggestions on pages 72–82 are for a variety of outdoor, gross-motor skills activities. These activities will allow students to explore a full range of motion: running, leaping, jumping, etc.

The final section of this book is devoted to journaling. The student journal gives students the opportunity to express their thoughts about the information presented in the activities and class discussions. It can be used for reflective writing, sorting or summarizing information, or to check for understanding.

Reproduce copies of the journal pages (83–93) for each student. You may wish to have students add pages to the journal throughout the year as new food and fitness topics arise. Students can add notebook paper to the journal, or you can reproduce extra copies of the blank journal pages (pages 92–93).

The CD includes ready-to-print PDF files of the student activity pages and the Food and Fitness Journal, as well as correlations to the Common Core State Standards and the National Health Education Standards.

Internet Resources

These sites provide useful, age-appropriate information to aid you in embarking on a year filled with active, healthy students. Let's move!

Action for Healthy Kids
This site provides information for schools, students, and parents, as well as programs to promote active, healthy lifestyles for kids.
http://www.actionforhealthykids.org/

CDC BAM! Body and Mind
This site was designed for 9–13-year-olds. BAM! provides information kids need to make healthy lifestyle choices.
http://www.cdc.gov/bam/teachers/index.html

Fresh for Kids
This site offers resources for kids and teachers, including informative pages on specific fruits and vegetables.
http://www.freshforkids.com.au/

Let's Move! America's Move to Raise a Healthier Generation of Kids
This program was developed by First Lady Michelle Obama to solve the epidemic of childhood obesity.
http://www.letsmove.gov/

National Farm to School Network
This site offers resources and information about farm-to-school programs in each state.
http://www.farmtoschool.org/

Nourish Interactive
This site offers free printable activities based on the *ChooseMyPlate.gov* food groups.
http://www.nourishinteractive.com/nutrition-education

Tips for Healthy Eating—Ten Healthy Habits for Kids
This site includes a summary of ways families can incorporate healthy eating habits.
http://www.nestle.com/nhw/health-wellness-tips/healthy-habits-kids

USDA—United States Department of Agriculture
This site includes kid-friendly research, printable materials, and Nutrition Fact Cards.
http://www.choosemyplate.gov/print-materials-ordering.html

The Whole Child
This site focuses on ensuring that each child in each school and in each community is healthy, safe, engaged, supported, and challenged to meet the demands of the 21st century.
http://www.wholechildeducation.org

Whole Grains Council
The Whole Grains Council wants to support everyone who's helping spread the word about the health benefits of whole grains, and about easy ways to find and enjoy more whole grains.
http://wholegrainscouncil.org/resources/educational-materials

National Health Education Standards

The activities in *Healthy Habits for Healthy Kids* (*Grades 1–2*) meet the following National Health Education Standards. For more information about these standards, go to *http://www.cdc.gov/healthyyouth/sher/standards/index.htm*

Standard 1. Students will comprehend concepts related to health promotion and disease prevention to enhance health.
Standard 1.2.1 Identify that healthy behaviors impact personal health.
Standard 1.2.2 Recognize that there are multiple dimensions of health.
Standard 1.2.3 Describe ways to prevent communicable diseases.
Standard 1.2.4 List ways to prevent common childhood injuries.
Standard 1.2.5 Describe why it is important to seek health care.
Standard 4. Students will demonstrate the ability to use interpersonal communication skills to enhance health and avoid or reduce health risks.
Standard 4.2.2 Demonstrate listening skills to enhance health.
Standard 4.2.3 Demonstrate ways to respond when in an unwanted, threatening or dangerous situation.
Standard 6. Students will demonstrate the ability to use goal-setting skills to enhance health.
Standard 6.2.1 Identify a short-term personal health goal and take action toward achieving the goal.
Standard 6.2.2 Identify who can help when assistance is needed to achieve a personal health goal.
Standard 7. Students will demonstrate the ability to practice health-enhancing behaviors and avoid or reduce health risks.
Standard 7.2.1 Demonstrate healthy practices and behaviors to maintain or improve personal health.
Standard 7.2.2 Demonstrate behaviors that avoid or reduce health risks.
Standard 8. Students will demonstrate the ability to advocate for personal, family, and community health.
Standard 8.2.2 Encourage peers to make positive health choices.

Common Core State Standards Correlation

The activities included in *Healthy Habits for Healthy Kids (Grades 1 and 2)* meet the following Common Core State Standards. (©Copyright 2010. National Governors Association Center for Best Practices and Council of Chief State School Officers. All rights reserved.) For more information, go to *http://www.corestandards.org/* or visit *http://www.teachercreated.com/standards/* for activities related to each standard.

Reading: Informational Text

Key Ideas and Details

ELA.RI.1.1 Ask and answer questions about key details in a text.

ELA.RI.1.2 Identify the main topic and retell key details of a text.

ELA.RI.2.3 Describe the connection between a series of historical events, scientific ideas or concepts, or steps in technical procedures in a text.

Craft and Structure

ELA.RI.1.4 Ask and answer questions to help determine or clarify the meaning of words and phrases in a text.

ELA.RI.2.4 Determine the meaning of words and phrases in a text relevant to a grade 2 topic or subject area.

Writing

Text Types and Purposes

ELA.W.1.2 Write informative/explanatory texts in which they name a topic, supply some facts about the topic, and provide some sense of closure.

ELA.W.2.2 Write informative/explanatory texts in which they introduce a topic, use facts and definitions to develop points, and provide a concluding statement or section.

Research to Build and Present Knowledge

ELA.W.1.8 With guidance and support from adults, recall information from experiences or gather information from provided sources to answer a question.

ELA.W.2.8 Recall information from experiences or gather information from provided sources to answer a question.

Speaking & Listening

Comprehension and Collaboration

ELA.SL.1.1 Participate in collaborative conversations with diverse partners about *grade 1 topics and texts* with peers and adults in small and larger groups.

ELA.SL.2.1 Participate in collaborative conversations with diverse partners about *grade 2 topics and texts* with peers and adults in small and larger groups.

ELA.SL.1.2 Ask and answer questions about key details in a text read aloud or information presented orally or through other media.

ELA.SL.2.2 Recount or describe key ideas or details from a text read aloud or information presented orally or through other media.

Presentation of Knowledge and Ideas

ELA.SL.1.5 Add drawings or other visual displays to descriptions when appropriate to clarify ideas, thoughts, and feelings.

ELA.SL.2.5 Create audio recordings of stories or poems; add drawings or other visual displays to stories or recounts of experiences when appropriate to clarify ideas, thoughts, and feelings.

ELA.SL.1.6 Produce complete sentences when appropriate to task and situation.

Language

Conventions of Standard English

ELA.L.1.1 Demonstrate command of the conventions of standard English grammar and usage when writing or speaking.

ELA.L.2.1 Demonstrate command of the conventions of standard English grammar and usage when writing or speaking.

ELA.L.1.2 Demonstrate command of the conventions of standard English capitalization, punctuation, and spelling when writing.

Vocabulary Acquisition and Use

ELA.L.1.4 Determine or clarify the meaning of unknown and multiple-meaning words and phrases based *on grade 1 reading and content,* choosing flexibly from an array of strategies.

ELA.L.2.4 Determine or clarify the meaning of unknown and multiple-meaning words and phrases based *on grade 2 reading and content,* choosing flexibly from an array of strategies.

ELA.L.2.5a Sort words into categories (e.g., *colors, clothing*) to gain a sense of the concepts the categories represent.

ELA.L.2.5a Identify real-life connections between words and their use (e.g., *describe foods that are spicy or juicy*).

ELA.L.1.6 Use words and phrases acquired through conversations, reading and being read to, and responding to texts, including using frequently occurring conjunctions to signal simple relationships (e.g., *because*).

ELA.L.2.6 Use words and phrases acquired through conversations, reading and being read to, and responding to texts, including using adjectives and adverbs to describe (e.g., *When other kids are happy that makes me happy*).

Take the Pledge

Directions: Read and practice the "Healthy Habits Pledge." When you are ready, recite it to a friend or family member. Sign your name at the bottom of the pledge when you have completed this activity and bring the page back to school.

Healthy Habits Pledge

I pledge to stay healthy and clean
through exercise and good hygiene.
I will eat balanced meals every day
to have more energy to learn and to play.
Every night I will get a good rest
to be more ready to do my best.
If I work hard to be healthy and strong
I'll be happier my whole life long.

I, _____, have read and learned the Healthy Habits Pledge.

- -

Directions: Write at least one personal health goal you would like to try this week. Choose from the following ideas. Later, as you learn more about healthy food choices and healthy habits, you may wish to write a goal more specific to your health needs.

- Choose servings the size of your fist.

- Have fruits and vegetables on half of your plate.

- Enjoy water as your favorite drink.

- Eat foods from each food group.

- Choose foods with less sugar and fat.

Week _____	Met	Not Yet
My personal goal this week is to _____ _____		

Challenge: Continue setting goals for yourself each week. Use the "My Personal Health Goals" in your journal (page 84) to help you keep track of each goal.

Introducing the 5 Food Groups

Healthy Habits for Healthy Kids refers to the five food groups listed on the USDA Choose My Plate site (*http://www.choosemyplate.gov.*). The table below lists foods in their true columns. See the notes below for exceptions for purposes of discussion with students.

Fruits

apples	grape juice	mangoes	plums
apple juice	grapefruit	nectarines	raisins
apricots	grapefruit juice	orange juice	raspberries
bananas	grapes	oranges	starfruit
blackberries	honeydew	papayas	strawberries
blueberries	kiwi fruit	peaches	tangerines
cantaloupe	lemons	pears	watermelon
cherries	limes	pineapples	

Vegetables

artichoke	carrots	lentils	spinach
asparagus	cauliflower	lima beans	split peas
bean sprouts	celery	mushrooms	sweet potatoes
beets	corn	navy beans	taro
black beans	eggplant	onions	turnips
black-eyed peas	garbanzo beans	peas	water chestnuts
bok choy	iceberg lettuce	pinto beans	wax beans
broccoli	kale	potatoes	white beans
Brussels sprouts	kidney beans	romaine lettuce	
cabbage	leaf lettuce	soybeans	

Culinary or Fruit Vegetables

avocados	green beans	green peppers	red peppers
cucumbers	pumpkins	squash	tomatoes

Important Distinctions

We define *fruit* as the sweet, fleshy part of a plant. Any part of a plant we eat that is *not* the fruit may be considered a vegetable. By this definition, vegetables can include *leaves, stems, roots, flowers, bulbs,* and *seeds.*

Culinary or Fruit Vegetables—We know that *fruit* refers to the flowering part of a plant in which seeds develop. By this definition, many foods we consider vegetables are actually fruits. Often, these foods are prepared or eaten as vegetables, so we call them "culinary vegetables" or "fruit vegetables."

Introducing the 5 Food Groups *(cont.)*

Grains	
Whole Grains	**Refined Grain Foods**

Whole Grains		Refined Grain Foods
amaranth	rolls	cereals
barley	rye	corn tortillas
brown rice	sorghum	cornbread
buckwheat	triticale	couscous
bulgar (cracked wheat)	whole grain cereal	crackers
cornmeal	whole wheat	flour tortillas
millet	whole wheat bread	grits
muesli	whole wheat crackers	noodles
oatmeal	whole wheat pasta	pasta
popcorn	whole wheat tortillas	pitas
quinoa	wild rice	white bread
rolled oats		white rice

Dairy

cheddar cheese	greek yogurt	parmesan cheese	Swiss cheese
cottage cheese	milk	pudding	yogurt
frozen yogurt	mozzarella cheese	ricotta cheese	

Protein

almonds	duck	lima beans	sesame seeds
beef	eggs	navy beans	soybeans
bison	fish	nuts	split peas
black beans	goose	peanuts	sunflower seeds
black-eyed peas	ham	pinto beans	turkey
cashews	hazelnuts	pork	veal
chicken	kidney beans	pumpkin seeds	venison
chickpeas	lamb	rabbit	walnuts

*Also ground beef, chicken, lamb, pork, turkey

Exercise of the Day

Here are some tips to get your daily indoor exercise program started.

1. Each day ask a student to choose a simple exercise movement from the list for the class to perform. Use the cards on pages 12 and 13.

2. Demonstrate the exercises as needed. When the movement involves stretching suggest slow and steady movements.

3. Ask questions that pertain to the movements.

   Run in Place!

   - How long can you make your arms or legs when you reach?

   - How fast can you run in place?

   - Can you run in slow motion?

   - When you pretend to climb a tree, do your hands and feet move together or do they alternate?

4. Set a timer or watch the clock and do the activity for one minute.

5. Have students add a tally mark for the chosen exercise to their "My Exercise Log" (page 85) in their journals each day after they have completed the action.

6. Repeat the same action throughout the day to signal transitions or simply to give students an opportunity to stretch and refocus their energies. Allow students to add additional tally marks each time in the day that they repeat the action.

Touch toes. Reach up.

Wiggle.

Hop on one foot.

"Exercise of the Day" Cards

Touch toes. Reach up.

Wiggle.

Hop on one foot.

Run in place.

Do jumping jacks.

Make large arm circles.

March in place.

Pretend to climb a mountain.

Do squats.

Do desk pushups.

Do chair squats.

Pretend to jump rope.

"Exercise of the Day" Cards *(cont.)*

Bicycle in chair.

Dance.

Do small arm circles.

Do leg raises.

Sway.

Bend and squat.

Neck rolls.

Shoulder scrunches.

Do tiptoe stretches.

Lean left, then right.

Lean forward, then back.

Pretend to hula hoop.

Fruits Checklist 1

Many fruits come from trees. They are different shapes and sizes. Put an **X** next to each fruit you have tried. Circle the ones you would like to try.

Citrus Fruits with Seeds

☐ grapefruit

☐ lemon

☐ lime

☐ orange

☐ tangerine

Fruits with Stones

☐ apricot

☐ cherry

☐ nectarine

☐ peach

☐ plum

More Fruits with Seeds

☐ apple

☐ pear

Fruits Checklist 2

Some fruits grow on trees. Others grow on plants, vines, or "runners" on the ground. They are different shapes and sizes. Put an **X** next to each fruit you have tried. Circle the ones you would like to try.

Berries

☐ blueberries

☐ grapes

☐ kiwi fruit

☐ raspberries

☐ strawberries

Tropical Fruits

☐ banana

☐ papaya

☐ mango

☐ pineapple

Melons

☐ cantaloupe

☐ honeydew

☐ watermelon

What Is a Fruit?

Fruit comes from the flowering part of a plant. It has the seeds for the plant. Some people think of fruit as a sweet part of a plant. Some fruits grow on trees. Other fruit grows on bushes or vines.

Fruits are healthy foods. They are important foods to eat. They have vitamins and minerals that help us stay strong and healthy. We should eat fruit every day.

Directions: Draw pictures of your favorite fruits. Label each fruit.

Fun Fact: Bananas come in more than one color. Did you know that there are red bananas?

Fruits That Grow on Trees

Fruit holds the seeds of a plant. Some seeds are small, but other seeds are large and are called stones. Some of these fruits grow on trees.

1. Some tree fruits have more than one seed inside. Count the number of seeds by 2s. Write the number of **seeds** you see next to each of these fruits that grow on trees.

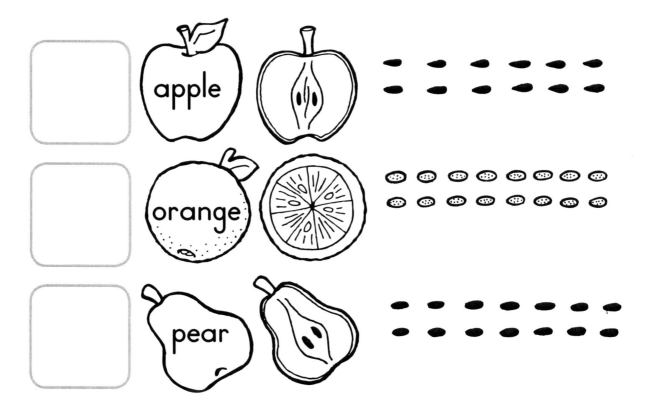

2. Other tree fruits only have one large seed called a **stone**. Color these stone fruits.

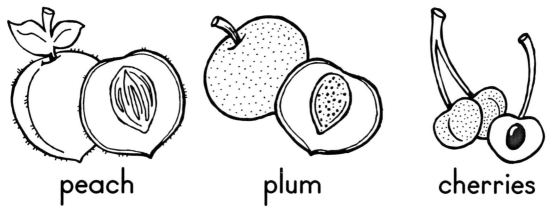

peach   plum   cherries

Fruits That Grow on Vines

Some fruits grow on vines. A vine is a plant with a long, twining stem. It grows along the ground or can climb a pole or fence.

1. Color these four fruits that grow on vines.

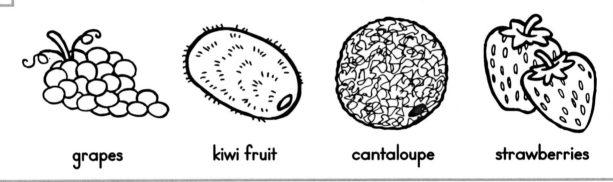

grapes   kiwi fruit   cantaloupe   strawberries

2. Trace the vine to find the fruit growing on it. Color the fruit.

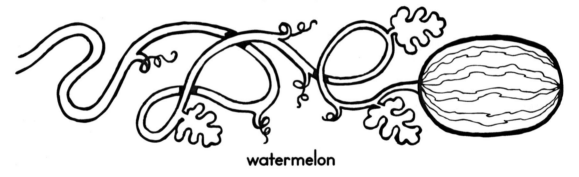

watermelon

3. Circle the name of the fruits on this vine. We sometimes call it a vegetable. Often we use it to make pie or bread.

pumpkin   cucumber   squash

Fun Fact: Strawberries are the only fruit whose seeds are on the outside!

Citrus Fruits

Some fruits are called **citrus** fruits. Oranges and grapefruits are round citrus fruits. Lemons and limes are oval in shape. Citrus fruits grow on trees in warm places. They are often made into juice or used to add flavor to foods. Citrus fruits give us vitamin C to keep us healthy.

1. Trace the shape of each fruit.

2. Color the inside and outside of each citrus fruit.

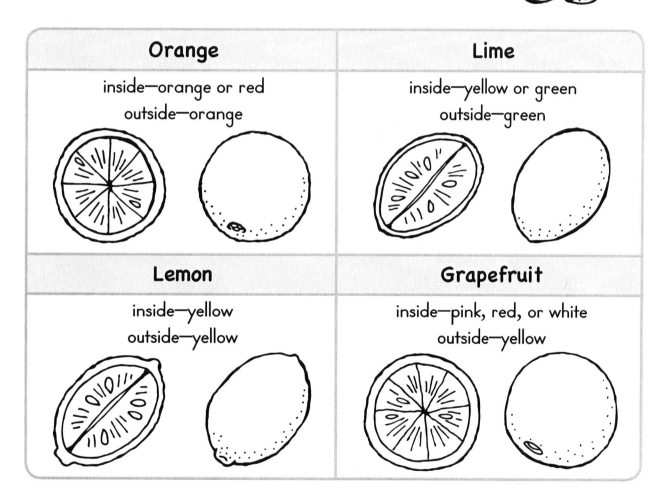

3. Put a check mark next to the citrus foods you eat or drink.

4. What vitamin do we get from all four citrus fruits? _____

Fun Fact: A full-grown orange tree can have over one thousand oranges each year.

A Rising Star

Starfruit is becoming better known in our country. When starfruit is sliced, it is shaped like a star. It has a sweet and sour taste. The fruit is juicy and crunchy. Some people say it tastes like a cross between an apple and a grape. Starfruit gives us vitamin C.

1. Count by **2s**, connect the dots, and learn what a starfruit looks like.

2. Color the starfruit green on the inside and yellow on the outside.

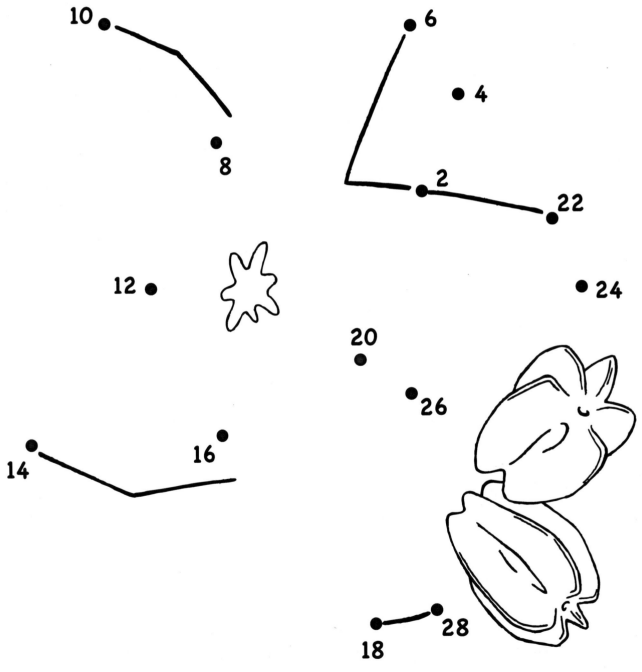

Favorite Fruits

We all have foods we like to eat. Many people like to eat fruit.

Look at the graph. The six fruits on the graph were liked the most by the students in Ms. Snyder's class.

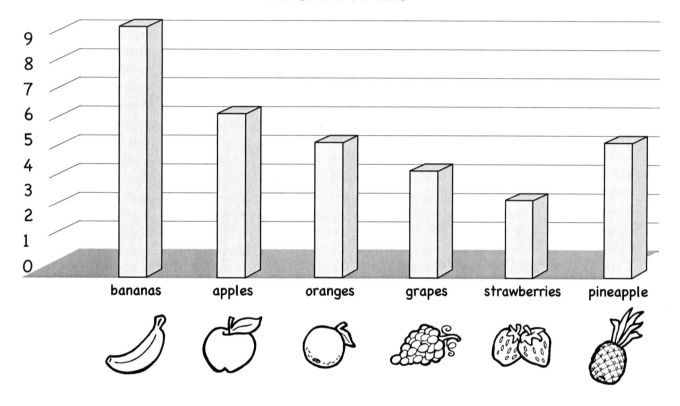

1. Which two fruits did students like the most?

_____ and _____

2. How many more students liked oranges than grapes? _____

3. How many students liked to eat strawberries? _____

4. What is your favorite fruit? _____

Fun Fact: It takes a pineapple plant two years to produce one fruit.

Which Juice Is Our Favorite?

Juice made from fruit can be a healthy food choice. Try to choose juice that does not have extra sugar in it. It is best to have juice once each day. Try to eat whole fruit other times during the day.

1. Take a vote in the classroom. Make a tally mark to show how many students like each kind of juice.

Favorite Juice	Tally	Total
orange juice		
apple juice		
grape juice		
cranberry juice		

2. Which juice was the class favorite? _____

3. Which juice is your favorite? _____

4. Which juice had the fewest tally marks? _____

Vegetables Checklist 1

We eat different parts of different vegetables. For some, we eat the *leaves* and for others the *roots* or *flowers*. How many of these vegetables have you tasted? Put an **X** by each one. Circle the ones you would like to try.

Leaf Vegetables

☐ cabbage

☐ chard

☐ kale

☐ lettuce

☐ spinach

Root Vegetables

☐ beets

☐ carrots

☐ daikon

☐ radishes

☐ turnips

Flower and Bud Vegetables

☐   ☐   ☐   ☐

artichoke   **asparagus**   **broccoli**   **cauliflower**

Name

Healthy Foods

Vegetables Checklist 2

Some vegetables grow in pods. Others have seeds like fruits, but we cook them like vegetables. How many of these vegetables have you tasted? Put an **X** by each one. Circle the ones you would like to try.

Vegetables in Pods

☐ green beans

☐ kidney beans

☐ lima beans

☐ peas

☐ pinto beans

☐ runner beans

☐ snow peas

☐ sugar snap peas

☐ wax beans

Culinary or Fruit Vegetables

☐ cucumber

☐ eggplant

☐ pumpkin

☐ tomato

☐ zucchini

Vegetables

A **vegetable** is a plant we grow to eat as food. It is important to eat a lot of vegetables. We eat different parts of vegetable plants. We eat the *leaves, stems, roots, flowers,* or *seeds* of different vegetables.

1. Read each sentence. Color the plants.

2. Circle the part of each vegetable plant that we eat.

---

1. We eat the **stem** of the celery plant.

2. We eat the **roots** of the carrot plant.

3. We eat the **leaves** of the lettuce plant.

4. We eat the **seed** of the sunflower.

5. We eat the **flowers** and **stem** of the broccoli plant.

Our Favorite Vegetables

Mrs. Kerr's class made a graph showing which vegetables they liked best.

Directions: Use the tally marks below to fill in the graph. The carrots have been done for you.

carrots	🥕	卌 I	6
corn	🌽	卌 IIII	9
cucumbers	🥒	III	3
green beans	🫘	卌	5
peas	🫛	II	2
lettuce	🥬	IIII	4

	carrots	corn	cucumbers	green beans	peas	lettuce
10						
9						
8						
7						
6						
5						
4						
3						
2						
1						

1. Which vegetable did the most students like? _____

2. Which vegetable did the fewest students like? _____

3. Did more kids like carrots or cucumbers? _____

4. Which of these vegetables do you like best? _____

Green Vegetables

There are many kinds of green vegetables. They are very important foods to eat. They have vitamins and minerals that help us stay strong and healthy. We should eat green vegetables every day.

Word Box		
asparagus	Brussels sprouts	kale
broccoli	peas	spinach

1. Write the name of each green vegetable on the line.

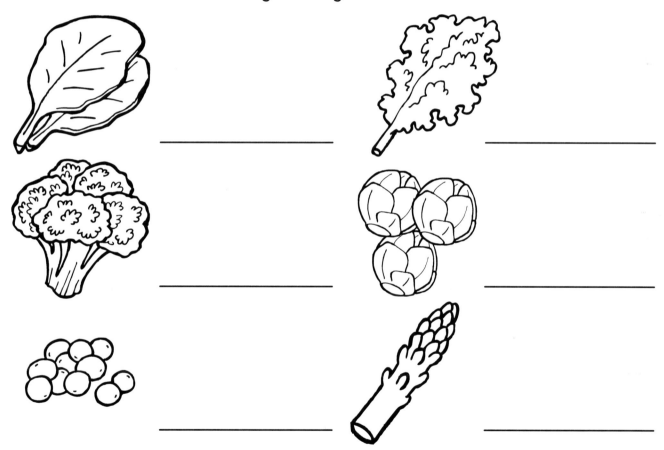

2. Circle all the vegetables whose leaves we eat.

3. Put boxes around the vegetables you have not tried yet.

Fun Fact: People in Egypt called asparagus the king of vegetables.

Hidden Green Beans

Green beans grow on bushes or vines. They have many names. Sometimes they are called string beans, and sometimes they are called French beans. Green beans are beans that can be eaten fresh or cooked.

1. Color the picture of the green beans.

2. How many green beans did you find?

Peppers

Why are some peppers green and some peppers red? Sometimes, green peppers are not picked right away. They stay on the vines longer. Then they turn red. A red pepper is a ripe green pepper. Other peppers turn orange or yellow when they are ripe. Red, orange, and yellow peppers taste sweeter than green peppers.

Directions: Use the Color Code to color the peppers.

Color Code
1 = green
2 = yellow
3 = orange
4 = red

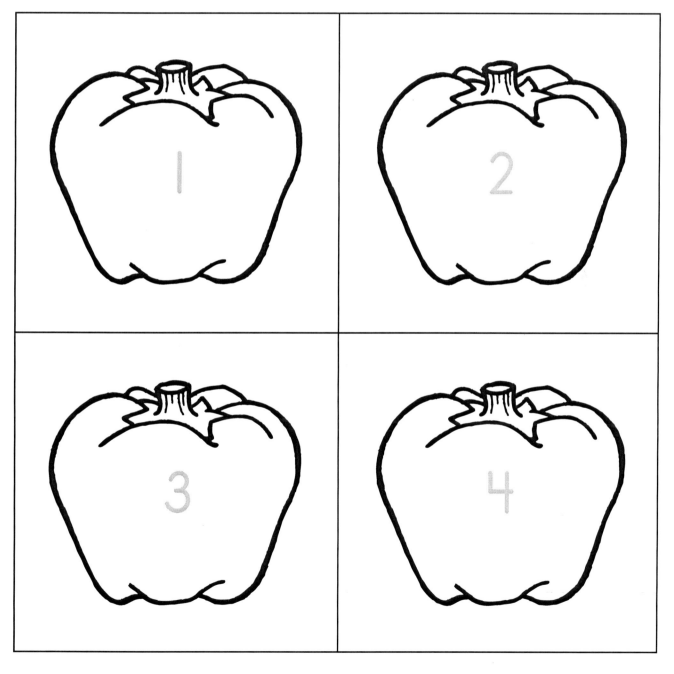

Colorful Vegetables

Vegetables come in many colors. Some come in more than one color.

Directions: Use the Word Box. Write the color of each vegetable on the line.

Word Box
blue   green   orange   purple   red   white   yellow

asparagus _____

beets _____

broccoli _____

cabbage _____

carrot _____

cauliflower _____

celery _____

eggplant _____

green beans _____

pepper _____

kale _____

lettuce _____

peas _____

potatoes _____

spinach _____

sweet potato _____

tomato _____

corn _____

1. Which color were the fewest vegetables? _____

2. Which color were the most vegetables? _____

Whole Grains Checklist

Oats, wheat, corn, barley, and rice are important grains. We eat them or use them to make flour to make breads, pasta, crackers, or tortillas. Circle the ones you have eaten. Draw a box around a grain food you might try.

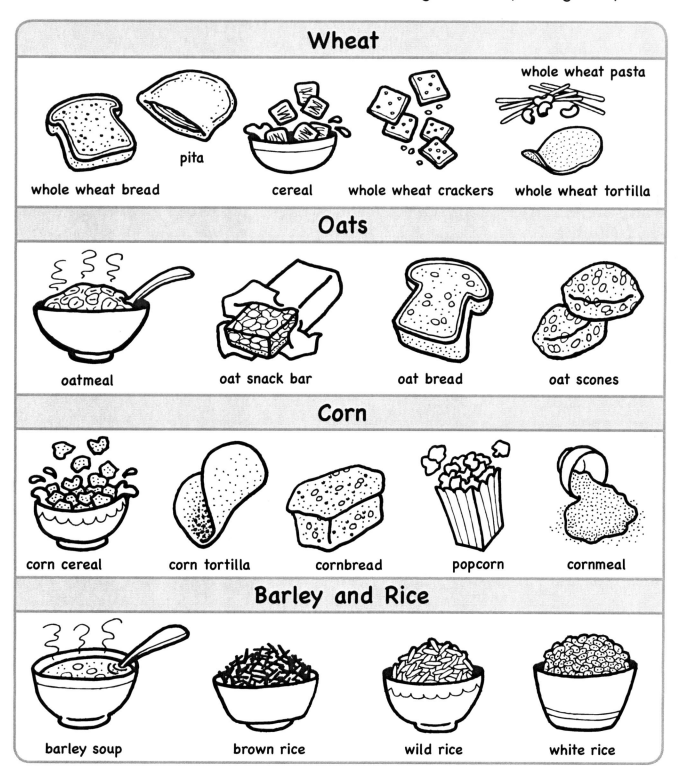

Wheat

whole wheat bread · pita · cereal · whole wheat crackers · whole wheat pasta · whole wheat tortilla

Oats

oatmeal · oat snack bar · oat bread · oat scones

Corn

corn cereal · corn tortilla · cornbread · popcorn · cornmeal

Barley and Rice

barley soup · brown rice · wild rice · white rice

Whole Grains

Grains grow in fields. Whole grains include the whole seed of the plant. The vitamins are found in the seed of the plant. Whole grains are a healthy food.

Directions: Cut out the pictures. Arrange them in order to show the steps to harvest grain. Glue them onto a piece of paper, label, and color them.

Whole Wheat Tic-Tac-Toe

Wheat is a grain. It is grown all around the world. There are many kinds.
Most wheat is ground into flour. One kind of wheat flour is used to make
bread. We use another kind of wheat flour for pasta. Many foods you eat
can be made with whole wheat flour.

1. Circle the pictures of foods that might be made with whole wheat flour.

2. Cross out the foods that would not be made with whole wheat flour.

3. Draw a line through the foods that are not made with the whole wheat
   flour. Did you win?

egg	bagels	bread
cereal	baked potato	crackers
pasta	tortillas	smoothie

Oats

Oats are a grain that grow in a field like wheat. Oats are harvested like wheat. Many people eat oats for breakfast.

Directions: Draw lines to match three ways to eat oats in the morning.

1.

When we cook oats, we can make oatmeal.

2.

We can eat toasted oat cereal with milk.

3.

Oat flour can be used to make bread for toast.

4. What is your favorite way to eat oats? _____
Draw a picture of it.

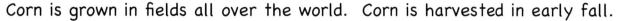

Corn

Corn is grown in fields all over the world. Corn is harvested in early fall.

- Fresh corn is a vegetable.

- Dried corn is a grain. It is ground into cornmeal. Muffins, corn bread, cereal, pancakes, and waffles can be made from cornmeal.

Sometimes in the fall, people make large mazes out of cornstalks after the corn has been picked. People can walk through these mazes. It is fun.

Directions: Find your way through the corn maze. Start at the corn muffins. Finish at the bowl of popcorn.

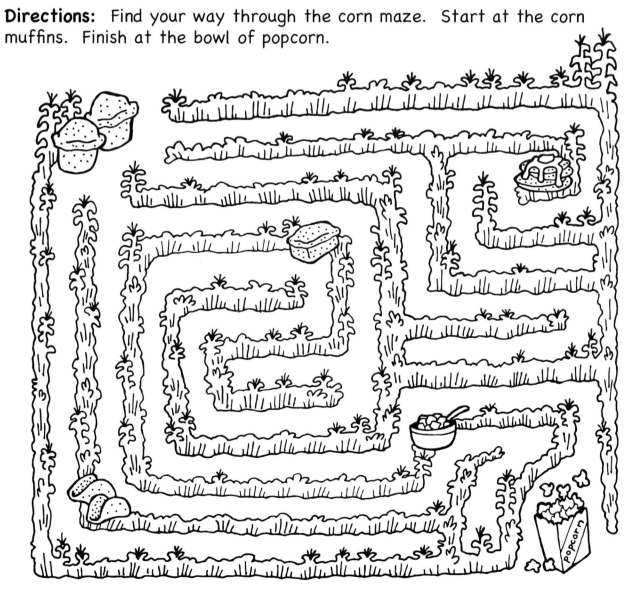

Circle the corn foods you pass in the maze. How many did you find? _____

Whole Grain Foods

Whole grain foods help our bodies grow healthy and strong. They have important nutrients. Common whole grains are **wheat**, **corn**, and **oats**. Some other whole grains are **popcorn**, **rye**, and **barley**.

Directions: Underline the whole grain word for each food below. Then, draw lines from the words to the matching foods in the column on the right.

1. rye bread

2. corn tortilla

3. oat cereal

4. popcorn

5. wheat crackers

6. beef barley soup

Dairy Foods Checklist

Dairy foods give us calcium to help us grow strong bones and teeth.

1. Put an **X** in the box near each dairy food you have tasted.
2. Circle the dairy foods you would like to try.

Dairy

☐ milk   ☐ yogurt   ☐ Greek yogurt

Cheeses

☐ string cheese

☐ parmesan

☐ cottage cheese

☐ cheddar   ☐ mozzarella   ☐ ricotta   ☐ swiss cheese

Dairy Treats

Some dairy products are treats. They are "sometimes" foods. They taste good, but it is best not to eat them every day.

☐ pudding   ☐ frozen yogurt   ☐ ice cream

Dairy Foods

Foods from the dairy group are made from milk. They give us calcium. Calcium helps us build strong bones and teeth.

Directions: Write the name of each dairy food next to its picture. Use the words in the Word Box to help you. Circle the dairy foods that are treats.

1. _____

2. _____

3. _____

4. _____

5. _____

6. _____

Word Box		
cheese	cottage cheese	ice cream
milk	pudding	yogurt

Name

Where Milk Comes From

Most of the milk we drink comes from cows. A dairy is a farm where dairy cows are raised to give milk. Other kinds of cows are raised to give meat.

Many years ago, farmers used their hands to milk each dairy cow. It took about 30 minutes to milk one cow. Today, most dairy cows are milked by machines. It takes about three minutes to milk a cow using a machine. It is much faster. Color the pictures of the cows being milked.

Fun Fact: Cream rises to the top of the milk when cows are milked. The cream can be used to make butter.

Say Cheese

Cheese is a dairy food. It is made from milk. There are different kinds of cheese. Some are hard, and some are soft. Some are white, some are yellow, and some have blue lines in them!

1. See what cheeses are the favorites in the class during whole-group time. Take a vote for each cheese below.

2. Write the total vote for each cheese in the box next to it.

cheddar cheese

string cheese

jack cheese

cottage cheese

swiss cheese

blue cheese

3. Which cheese got the most votes? _____

4. Which cheese got the fewest votes? _____

5. What is your favorite cheese? _____

6. Which cheese would you like to try? _____

Fun Fact: Cheese can also be made from goat's milk or milk from sheep.

Name

Dairy or Not?

Look at the foods in each row. Some are dairy foods and some are from other food groups.

Directions: Cross out the food in each row that is not a dairy food.

Row 1

Row 2

Row 3

Row 4

Dairy Foods for Every Meal

Dairy foods are important foods. Each meal below is missing its dairy food.

1. Cut out the dairy foods at the bottom of the page.

2. Add a dairy food to each meal or snack.

3. Discuss your choices with classmates. Did everyone make the same choices? _____

4. What are two of your favorite foods from the dairy group?

_____ _____

5. What dairy food would you have with dinner? _____

Protein Foods Checklist

Directions: Circle each protein food you have tasted. Put a box around one food you might try.

Poultry and Eggs

goose   turkey   eggs   chicken   duck

Nuts, Seeds, and Legumes

pumpkin seeds   almonds   peanuts

sunflower seeds   hazelnuts   sesame seeds   walnuts   cashews

Beans and Peas

split peas   navy beans

lima beans   pinto beans

black beans   black-eyed peas   kidney beans   chickpeas

Meats

lamb

beef (cow)   rabbit   bison   ham (pig)   venison (deer)

Protein Foods

Protein is found in foods we eat. We get most of our protein from meat, eggs, and fish. We can also get protein from seeds and nuts. There is protein in dairy foods, too, like milk.

Some people call protein the building blocks of our bodies. That's because protein helps us build strong muscles. Protein also helps us make red blood cells to help us breathe.

1. Color the protein foods in each block.

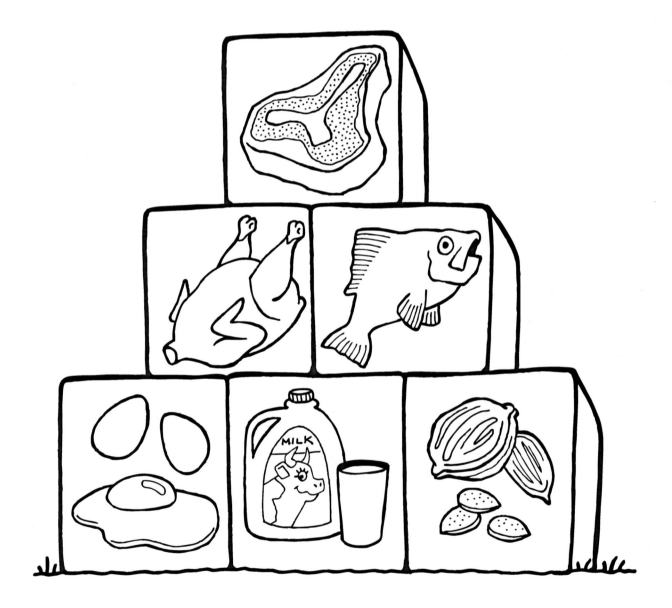

2. Which protein food do you eat most often? _____

Animals Give Us Protein

Some animals provide foods that are good for us. Match the animals below to the protein foods they give us. Color the page.

Can you think of other foods from these animals?

Cow _____   **Fish** _____

Chicken _____   **Pig** _____

Legumes

Legumes are protein foods. They are also vegetables that grow on vines or bushes. Legumes can be eaten many different ways.

Directions: Use the circle chart above to help you answer the questions.

1. Which legumes could be put in salad? _____

2. Which legume makes a great vegetable dip? _____

3. Which legume could you eat fresh from the garden? _____

4. Which legumes makes a tasty soup on a cold day? _____

5. Which legume makes a yummy sandwich spread? _____

Peanuts Are Legumes

Peanuts are legumes, but we eat them like nuts. Peanuts give us protein. A peanut plant looks like a bush above ground. It has flowers that send "pegs" down into the ground. Peanuts grow underground, which is why they are called "groundnuts." They do not grow on trees like other nuts.

1. Color the peanut bush green. Color the peanuts tan.

2. Count the peanuts growing underground. How many peanuts did you find?

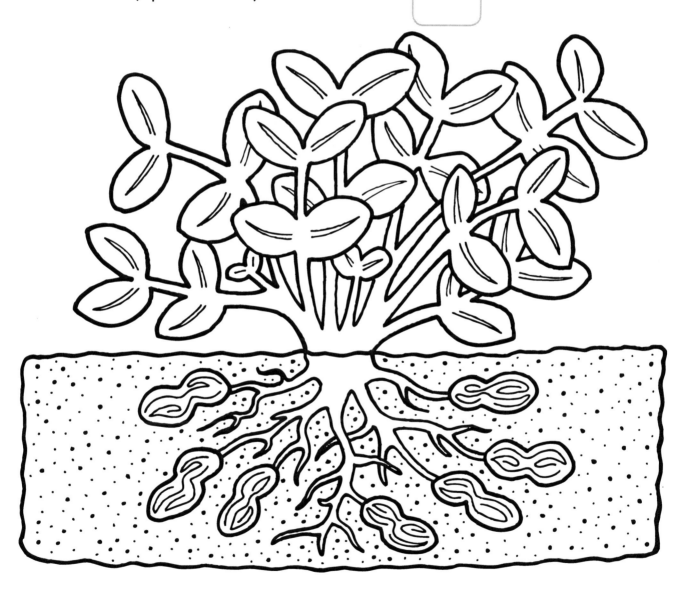

Fun Fact: Peanuts are brain food.

Nuts We Eat

Nuts are healthy foods. Nuts have protein and are a good snack food. They give us energy. They are especially good for us when eaten raw. The hard part is getting them out of their shells. Often, nuts are added to salads, breads, and stuffing.

1. Look at each nut. Have you ever eaten it? Circle **yes** or **no**.

Almond		yes	no
Hazelnut		yes	no
Pecan		yes	no
Pine nuts		yes	no
Pistachio		yes	no
Walnut		yes	no

2. Circle the tools that might be good to use to get a nut out of its shell.

3. Describe how you would get a nut out of its shell. _____

_____

Fun Fact: Almonds have more calcium than any other nut. They are great for our health.

Tree Nuts

Walnuts and almonds are two kinds of nuts that grow on trees. On the trees, these nuts are hidden in greenish hulls. They have to be taken out of the hulls and then out of their shells before they can be eaten.

1. How many walnuts can you see growing on the branch?

2. Color the walnut hulls green.

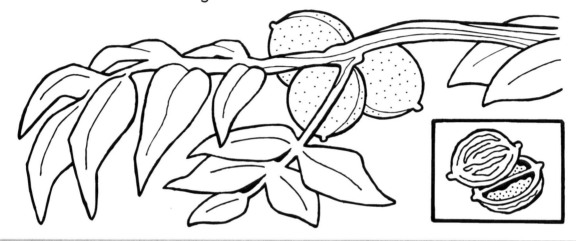

3. How many almonds can you find on the branch?

4. Color the almond hulls green.

5. Write a sentence about a nut you have eaten.

_____

_____

_____

Good Nutrition Is Important

Good nutrition is important. We have learned about healthy foods in each of the food groups. We know that healthy foods are important to eat. They give us things we need to grow and stay healthy like vitamins and minerals.

1. Name one food from each of the 5 food groups.

    Fruits: _____

    Vegetables: _____

    Grains: _____

    Protein: _____

    Dairy: _____

2. Draw fruits and vegetables on half the plate.
3. Add a protein food to the plate.
4. Add your favorite grain food to the plate.
5. What dairy food or drink would be good with this meal? Add it.
6. What is something you have learned about nutrition?

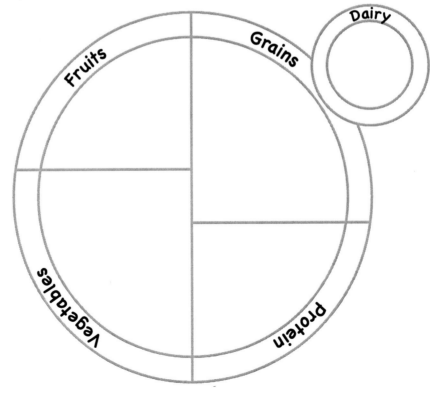

"Sometimes" Foods

It is important to eat healthy foods at every meal. But sometimes we enjoy treats. Think of treats as "sometimes" foods. Sometimes foods are special treats for special times. Read the poem below and discuss what it means.

"Sometimes" Foods

"Sometimes" foods
are a special treat.
Some are salty
and some are sweet.

They are yummy
and can make you smile.
But only eat them
once in a while!

Eat healthy foods
to learn and grow.
And you'll be happy,
don't you know!

1. Name some *salty* treats.

   _____   _____

   _____   _____

2. Name some *sweet* treats.

   _____   _____

   _____   _____

3. What is your favorite treat? _____

Riddle Time

Guess the answers to these riddles. Color the two pictures in each row that fit the clues.

1. Which foods are called vegetables but are really fruits?
   Hint: They have seeds on the inside.

2. Which foods grow underground?

3. Which foods hide inside hard shells?

4. Which foods can "swim" in water?

5. Which foods hide seeds inside?

6. Which foods are made from grasses?

Making Good Food Choices

People eat different foods in different parts of the world. We do not all choose the same foods to eat. We cannot all grow the same kinds of foods. Our friends might eat things we have not tried before.

1. Draw a picture of a meal you had yesterday or today. It could be breakfast, lunch, or dinner.

2. Use a _blue_ crayon to circle your favorite food.

3. Use a _green_ crayon to circle the healthiest food.

4. Trade papers with a partner. Use a _red_ crayon or pencil to circle the food on your partner's plate that you might like to try.

Find the Healthy Foods

1. Find the healthy foods in this puzzle. The words may go **forward, backward,** or **diagonally.** Work with a friend.

2. Color the letter boxes for each word as you find it.

m	s	a	e	p	b	m	h	y	l
t	e	h	r	c	u	a	e	o	d
h	k	s	a	f	n	k	s	g	m
r	a	p	f	y	r	o	l	u	a
i	c	i	j	u	i	c	e	r	k
c	n	o	t	a	t	o	p	t	c
w	a	t	e	r	m	e	l	o	n
z	p	l	t	g	s	p	u	k	u
a	f	p	e	a	c	h	m	b	t
e	s	e	e	h	c	r	a	o	s

Word Box

cheese
juice
muffin
nuts
pancakes
peach
peas
plum
potato
turkey
watermelon
yogurt

3. Which foods would you like to eat for breakfast? _____

_____

4. Which foods would you eat for a healthy snack? _____

_____

Hidden Message

Write the name of each food next to its picture. Use the words in the word box to help you. Write one letter in each box. The letters in the dark boxes will spell a mystery word. Write the mystery word on the line at the bottom of the page.

1. ☐ ☐ ☐ ☐ ☐ ☐

2. ☐ ☐ ☐ ☐

3. ☐ ☐ ☐ ☐ ☐

4. ☐ ☐ ☐ ☐ ☐ ☐ ☐

5. ☐ ☐ ☐ ☐ ☐ ☐

6. ☐ ☐ ☐ ☐ ☐

7. ☐ ☐ ☐ ☐ ☐ ☐

Word Box

apple	lettuce	peach	turkey
cheese	oatmeal	peas	

Mystery Word: _____

Keeping Our Food Safe

Keeping our food safe is important. Here are some things to remember:

- Wash your hands before eating.

- Use clean dishes, pots, and cooking items.

- Foods like milk should be kept cold. Others should not be eaten unless they are cooked, like most meat.

- Fruits and vegetables from the garden or the store can be eaten after they are washed. They do not need to be cooked.

1. Look at each picture. Discuss how the actions keep food safe to eat.

2. Describe what is happening in each picture. Use the lines in each box.

1.

2.

3.

4.

Things We Do to Stay Healthy

Directions: Unscramble the words below to find healthy habits. Use the picture clues.

1. u b h r s   e h t e t

_____

2. r s e i x e c e

_____

3. n d k i r   r e a w t

_____

4. t a e   s a f r t a b k e

_____

5. e p l e s

_____

6. s a w h   s h a d n

_____

Wash Your Hands

Washing your hands is an important healthy habit. Think about all the things you touch in a day that other people also touch. You can't **see** the germs on those things, but they are there. Sometimes germs can make you sick. You can keep the germs AWAY by washing your hands.

It is good to wash your hands:

- before meals
- after using the bathroom
- after playing outside
- after playing with a pet
- after you sneeze or cough

1. Cut out the pictures below. Put them in order to show the correct way to wash your hands. Glue the pictures to a piece of paper.

2. Write a sentence or two on the new page telling about when you wash your hands.

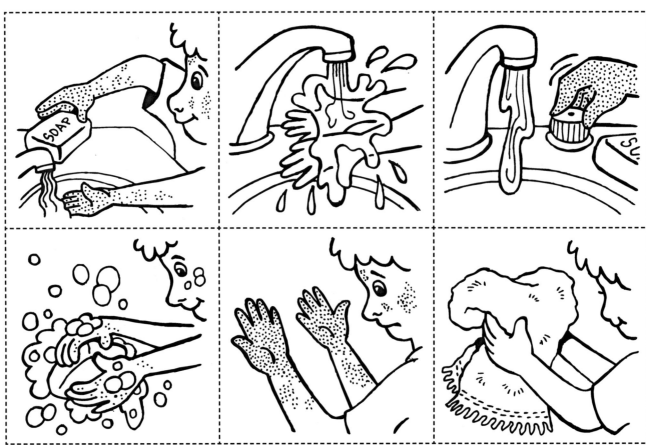

Take Care of Yourself

When we get sick it is important to take care of ourselves. This helps us to get well again. It also keeps other people from getting sick. It is important to try not to spread germs.

1. Circle two things that will help you get better when you get sick.

Getting rest.   Drinking water.   Exercise.

2. Talk about the pairs of pictures below. Cross out the picture in each row that shows a child spreading germs. Circle the picture that shows the child who is not spreading germs.

Row 1
Sharing a drink.   Drinking your own drink.

Row 2
Washing eyes with a clean cloth.   Rubbing eyes.

Row 3
Coughing into hands.   Coughing into elbow.

Healthy Teeth

Teeth are important. They let us smile. Our teeth help us chew our food. Teeth help us talk. We want to keep our teeth clean to keep them healthy. We don't want to get **cavities**.

When we are born we do not have teeth. We can't chew foods. Our first teeth are called baby teeth. Baby teeth fall out when we are about 7 years old. This leaves room for new teeth to grow. We call the new teeth **permanent teeth**. They are bigger and have to last a long time.

1. Draw your smile.

   Are you missing any teeth?

   Yes   No

   If so, how many?

2. Circle the things you can use to keep your teeth clean.

3. List four healthy foods you can eat because you can chew.

   _____   _____   _____   _____

4. Color the foods below. These foods help your teeth stay healthy. Circle the one you like the best.

cheese   chicken   nuts   milk

Inside a Tooth

Every tooth is made up of different parts. The **crown** is the part of your tooth that you can see.

The **root** is the part of your tooth that is in your gum. It holds your tooth in your mouth.

There are different parts inside your tooth. Look at the diagram below.

- The inside part of a tooth is called the **pulp**. It has blood vessels so the tooth can receive nutrients. It also has nerves so that you can feel your tooth.

- The **dentin** is a yellow, bone-like material. It contains nerves. The nerves hurt if there is a problem with your tooth.

- The **enamel** is the hard white covering of a tooth. We brush the enamel of our teeth to keep it strong. It protects the inside of the tooth.

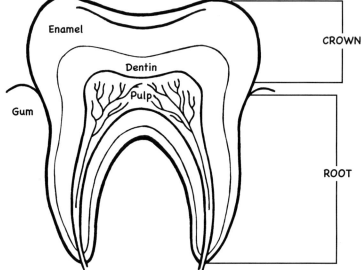

1. Color the **pulp** inside the tooth red.

2. Color the **dentin** around the pulp yellow.

3. Color the **gums** around the **root** pink. Pink gums are healthy gums.

4. Which part of the tooth do you see when someone smiles?

   _____

5. Which two parts of the tooth have nerves so that you can feel when something is wrong?

   _____   _____

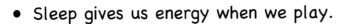

Sleep Is Good for Us

We need rest each day to stay healthy. A good night's sleep gives our bodies time to rest.

- Sleep gives us energy when we play.

- Sleep helps us do better in school.

- Sleep keeps us from getting sick.

- Sleep helps us feel rested and make good choices.

How much sleep do we need? Children need about 10 hours of sleep each day. Here are some suggestions for healthy sleep:

- Do something active every day, outside if you can.

- Eat healthy foods. Don't eat a lot of sweets.

- Read or listen to a story before bedtime.

- Turn off the TV or computer.

- Go to bed at the same time every night.

1. Write two things you do to get a good night's sleep each night.

_____

_____

2. What time do you get up in the morning? Draw hands on the clock to show the time.

3. Count backwards ten hours from the time you get up. Draw hands on the clock to show a healthy bedtime.

Stay Safe

There are many ways to stay safe. Here are some important rules:

- Look both ways before going into the street. Cross at a crosswalk.
- Wear a helmet to ride a bike, a scooter, or a skateboard.
- Look to see if something is safe to touch before touching it.
- Follow safety rules on the playground and at the swimming pool.

1. Look at the pictures. Discuss which pictures show ways to stay safe.

2. Cross out the pictures that are not safe ideas.

Stranger Danger

Sometimes people talk to us when we are away from home. We might know the person, and we might not. A **stranger** is someone we do not know. Many times we are with a parent or a trusted grownup. Someone might say hello to us. If we are with a grownup we know, then it is okay to say hello. That is the polite thing to do.

If someone wants to talk to us or take us somewhere, we should walk right back to the safe grownup we know. Sometimes we are not with a trusted grownup. We might be walking to school. Then it is not safe to talk to someone we do not know. It is not safe to take things from people we do not know. We should not go somewhere with someone we do not know.

Directions: Read each sentence together. Decide if it is a safe thing to do. If it is safe, draw a smiley face ☺ in the box. Discuss all answers.

1.	You are at the doctor's office with a parent. The person at the desk offers you a sticker. Is it safe to take the sticker and say thank you?	
2.	You are walking to the school bus stop in the morning. A grownup you do not know asks for directions. Is it safe to talk to the person?	
3.	You are playing at the beach. A grownup family member is sitting there watching you. The parent of a child playing nearby asks you where to find the bathroom. Is it safe to answer the question?	
4.	You are playing outside in your front yard. The neighbor next door asks if your dad is home. You know they are friends. Is it safe to answer the question?	
5.	You are walking to your friend's house to play. A man walking his dog says hello. You have never seen him before. Is it safe to talk to him?	

Bones Need Calcium

Think about your skeleton. It is made of bones. The bones are hard, and they are strong. Bones and teeth need calcium to stay strong and healthy. We get calcium from these healthy foods. They are good for our bodies.

milk, yogurt, cheese   soy milk   sardines

tofu   salmon   collard greens

Why do we need bones? What do bones do for our bodies?

- Bones give our bodies shape. They allow us to stand up tall and sit comfortably.
- Bones protect our organs. They are strong shields for our brains, hearts, and lungs.
- Bones help us move.

1. Without bones, what would you look like? _____

2. Look at the foods above. Name two foods you eat to help grow strong

   bones. _____ _____

3. What do strong bones help you do? _____

Bones, No Bones

Stand and move in different ways. Focus on how different joints help you move. Discuss what movements our ankles, knees, and elbows (joints) allow us to do. Then, play a game like **Freeze**. Choose someone to be the leader. While others are moving about, the leader will call out, "No Bones." Everyone moving must act like they have no bones. Keep playing, switching leaders from time to time.

No bones!!!

Being Active

Active means moving. There are many ways to be active. Think about the things you do when you play each day.

  1. Write a list of active words (verbs) that describe what you like to do.

_____   _____

_____   _____

_____   _____

  2. Draw a picture of yourself being active.

Did You Stretch Today?

Stretching is good for us. Stretching is a form of exercise you can do every day, inside or outside. You don't need any equipment! It helps us move better, and it helps us breathe better. Sometimes doing a few stretches helps us concentrate better, too.

It is best to move around a little before you stretch. This warms up the muscles. Then when you stretch you will not get hurt. Here are some tips to stretch carefully:

- Breathe deeply while you stretch.
- Don't bounce. Hold each stretch for a few seconds.
- Stretch both sides of your body equally.

Directions: Try the following stretches before exercising.

1.	Raise your arms and reach toward the ceiling. Lean to the left, then lean to the right. Move slowly. Feel the stretch. 
2.	Stand with your arms out, like you are making a "T." Make large circles with your arms. Slowly go forward five or six times. Then, make the same circles going in the opposite direction. Next, try making smaller and smaller circles in each direction. 
3.	Do slow lunges. Bend one knee so that it is right above your ankle. Stretch the other leg out behind you. Don't bounce, just hold the lunge for a count of ten and then switch legs. Can you hold your arms up while you are lunging? 
4.	Sit on the floor with your legs spread apart. Place both hands in between your legs and lean forward gently. Don't bounce. Move slowly toward one foot, then back to the middle, and then toward the other foot. Do this stretch three or four times. 

Daily Movements

We do chores and other tasks at home and at school. We move in different ways when we do these things.

Look at each picture. Discuss what each person is doing. Then look at the word box. Find action words that describe the movements the person does to complete the task. You may use words more than once. The first one is done for you.

1. _____ bend, stretch, pull _____

2. _____

3. _____

4. _____

5. _____

6. _____

Word Box

balance	carry	pull	reach	sway
bend	lift	push	stretch	walk

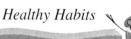

Playing with Movement

There are many ways to move. Dancing is a way to move and stay active. You can act like animals or plants when you dance. You can use moves from different sports, too!

Think and Discuss

- Think about grain growing in a field. How does it move?
- What is your favorite animal? How does it move?
- What sport do you like to play? How do you move when you play that sport?

Act It Out

Have students work together in small groups to create a sequence of 4 or 5 moves that others can follow.

1. Each person in the group can choose one move to act out.
2. Take turns demonstrating each move.
3. As a group, decide the order of the moves. Practice the moves in order.
4. Take turns sharing each group's moves with the class.
5. Add music if you can. Does music make a difference in the movements?

Examples of Movement Sequences

Direct students to carry out the following sequences:

Grain in Field—Sway slowly back and forth, move faster, stop with hands reaching overhead, bend and touch toes, repeat.

Monkey—Pretend to climb up a tree (arm over arm 3 times), swing arms back and forth as if swinging to a vine (2 times), squat, and pretend to eat.

Baseball—Swing like a batter (3 times), run in place, jump and reach up to catch a ball, throw the ball.

Animal Moves

Teacher Directions: Discuss the many different ways animals move. Think about each animal below. How does it move? How does it get food? How does it protect itself? Invite students to take turns moving like each animal. Try playing Charades using the featured animals.

Student Directions: Describe how each animal moves. You may use the Word Box to help you fill in the blanks.

Word Box
crawl
climb
dig
flap
hop
leap
reach
run
slither
swim
swing

1. Can you _____ like a lizard?

2. Can you _____ like a fish?

3. Can you _____ a hole for a bone like a dog?

4. Can you _____ fast like a cheetah?

5. Can you _____ like a snake?

6. Can you _____ like a rabbit?

7. Can you _____ like a monkey?

8. Can you _____ up to get some leaves to eat like a giraffe?

9. Can you _____ your wings very fast like a hummingbird?

10. Can you _____ out of the water like a whale?

Simon Says

Teacher Directions: Play Simon Says with students. Be the leader until students are comfortable with the movement options. Remind students that if you don't say "Simon Says...." before the action you want them to do, they should not move. Only move when "Simon" says to do something!

Here is how a game might start:

Simon says, "Wiggle in place." ➜ *Students wiggle.*

Simon says, "Hop on one foot." ➜ *Students hop.*

"Dance in place." ➜ *Students do **not** dance, since* <u>Simon</u> *did not say to.*

Simon says, "Run in place." ➜ *Students run in place.*

Simon says, "Hop on 2 feet." ➜ *Students hop.*

"Stop!" ➜ *Students do **not** stop, since* <u>Simon</u> *did not say to.*

Simon says "Stop!" ➜ *Students stop moving.*

Movements for Indoor Version

Raise your arms.	Slide to the left or to the right!
Hands on your head, waist, or knees.	March in place.
Hop on two feet.	Lean to the left.
Hop on one foot.	Lean to the right.
Freeze!	Wiggle in place.

Movements for Outdoor Version

Crab-walk 6 steps.

Take 3 giant steps forward or backward.

Do arm circles. (pick a number of times)

Dance in place.

Run to _____ and come back.
  (give destination)

Move backward or forward taking baby steps. (pick a number of steps)

What other movements can you think of to have your classmates try?

Ideas for Outdoors

Start with these transitions to go in and out of the classroom. Explain that each day the class will walk out one way and come back into the classroom doing the opposite movements. Here are a few suggestions to get started:

- Walk outside on heels, walk inside on toes.
- Walk outside quickly, walk inside slowly.
- Walk outside going forward, walk backward or sideways to return to the classroom.
- Slouch walking out, stand tall walking back in.
- Walk outside with arms in front, walk inside with arms behind back.
- Walk outside in a straight line, walk into the room in a curvy line.

Relay Races

Place a line of tape or string on the floor (or ground) for each team. Introduce a number of ways to go from Start to Finish. Start with these:

- Hop back and forth over the line (zig-zagging) from Start to Finish. Sit down when all teammates have hopped back and forth to the finish.
- Team members stand on the line. Pass a beanbag or other small object alternating over head and under legs to the end of the line and back again. Sit down when item is back at the start.

Skill Development

Teach students gross motor skills, such as galloping, leaping, and skipping.

Galloping: Have students hold hands and slide around the circle. Then have students drop hands and turn in the direction the circle is moving. They continue to slide, now moving forward; remind children they'll pick up their feet a little more. Try pretending to be horses.

Leaping: Find a grassy or sandy place to practice. Have students take a few running steps before they leap. Have students try to leap as far as they can. Alternatively, ask them to imagine they are leaping over a low step or wall. If you wish, have students participate in leaping contests for distance and height.

Skipping: Have students step and then hop on one foot. Then ask them to take a step and hop with the next foot. Suggest that students swing their arms as they skip to help them maintain balance and rhythm. Invite students to sing a song as they skip.

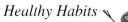

Outdoor Activities Using Props

Scarf Tosses

Use old scarves or 12" squares of fabric. Have students follow a series of directions using the scarves. To start, allow students ample time to practice tossing the scarves up and catching them before they hit the ground. Encourage students to toss the scarves up as high as they can and then let them float down.

Then, try the following ideas:
- Toss the scarf with the left hand and catch it with the right hand. Then switch hands and catch the scarf with the left hand.
- Toss the scarf up high, turn around once, and try to catch the scarf before it floats to the ground.
- Toss and catch the scarf with a partner.

Beach Ball Toss

Tossing, bouncing, and catching a beach ball is fun and good exercise that can be done outside or seated as a classroom activity. Why not combine activity with a skills practice? Take a few minutes to label the ball with words, letters, or numbers.

1. Have students arrange themselves in a circle.
2. Explain to students that they will toss the beach ball back and forth until they hear a signal.
3. The student who has the ball at the signal will read the word, letter, or number written on the ball that is closest to his or her right thumb.

Consider writing on beach balls using permanent ink.
Students can practice one of the following skills:
- letter identification
- sight words
- word recognition
- rhyming with the word on the ball
- addition facts or subtraction facts

Ball Rolling

Rolling a ball involves a number of skills including eye-hand coordination. To start, have students sit in a circle with legs crossed. Have each student practice rolling and catching the ball across the circle.

Outdoor Activities Using Props (cont.)

Bowling

Use a medium-sized ball and six 2-liter bottles as bowling pins for each lane of bowling. Use chalk or tape to suggest bowling lanes.

Teacher Note: Depending on the strength of the students and the weight of the ball, you may wish to add some sand or other material to weigh down the "pins."

How to Play

1. Arrange the pins in a triangle.

2. Use a marker or piece of tape to establish a starting point for the "bowler."

3. Have students take turns standing behind the marker and rolling the ball to knock over the pins.

4. Explain that the goal is to knock over as many pins as possible. This may be done in one turn, or students may be given a second roll, just as in regular bowling.

5. Engage other students to be in charge of ball retrieval and pin set-up to keep the game moving and more students involved.

Kicking

Use a piece of wadded-up newspaper for kicking practice. (Let students do the "wadding.") The newspaper ball will stand still more readily than a real ball. Once students are comfortable kicking the newspaper balls, try some of these activities:

- Create a target into which the students must kick the "ball." (A large box works well.)

- Kick the ball back and forth between partners.

- Draw chalk lines, and see if students can kick the ball along the lines. Try relay races along the lines.

Teacher Note: Incorporate real balls and longer distances for targets as students' kicking skills improve.

Human Obstacle Course

You can make an obstacle course without any equipment! Divide students into two groups. One group will form an obstacle course. The other group will go through the course. Then the groups will switch.

Here are some ideas for "obstacles." Use them all, or try just a few to start.

1. Form a tunnel for others to crawl or walk through.
   (pairs of students)

2. Hold hands with a classmate to make a low log for someone to step over. (pair of students)

3. Hold hands with a classmate to make an arch for someone to walk under. (pair of students)

4. Have 4 or 5 classmates stand in an uneven row to make "gates" like skiers use. Others will zig-zag back and forth to go through the gates.

5. Ask students to think of other "obstacles" to add.

Catch, Throw, and Kick

Catching and throwing objects are skills we learn. We use our eyes, hands, and feet together. Spend time practicing these skills with students. Here are some pointers to share with them:

Throwing — Hold the ball in your hand. Look in the direction of the "catcher" and aim the ball toward them as you throw. This makes it easier for the other person to catch the ball.

Catching — Watch the ball. Keep your eye on the ball. Move your feet and hands toward the ball to help you catch it.

1. Have students practice throwing and catching with a partner. Use a soft ball or make a ball out of crumpled paper. As skills improve, move students farther back from each other to throw and catch.

2. Practice new skills in different ways. Ask,

   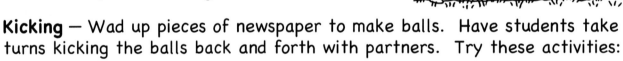

   - How far can you throw the ball?

   - How many times can you throw the ball?

   - Can you hit a target with the ball?

Kicking — Wad up pieces of newspaper to make balls. Have students take turns kicking the balls back and forth with partners. Try these activities:

- Kick the ball along a line. Make a line on the floor with tape, or draw a chalk line outside.

- Make a finish line at one end of a play area. Line up with balls at the other end of the play area. Walk or run while kicking the balls. Race with classmates to see who can reach the finish line first.

- Create an obstacle course with rows of cones or boxes. Take turns going through the obstacle course while kicking the balls.

Extension: Have students create a chart naming sports in which each skill is used.

Throwing	Catching	Kicking

Fitness Fun

Try some of these games to get students to be active while thinking about healthy foods and habits.

Color Bounce

1. Pair up the students.
2. Each pair will use a small bouncy ball, a piece of crumpled paper from the recycling bin, or a beanbag.
3. The first person will toss the ball to his or her partner, naming a color.
4. The partner must return the toss, naming a healthy food that is that color.
5. Repeat with different colors and foods. Take turns saying colors and foods.

Fast or Slow

1. Play a game similar to *Red Light, Green Light*.
2. The leader calls out a healthy food or a "sometimes food" (treat).
3. Players may walk quickly when a healthy food is called.
4. Players should move in slow motion when they hear a "sometimes food" is called.
5. Switch leaders after four or five movements.

Color Food Relay

1. Divide the class into four groups. Assign each group a color category: red, orange and yellow, green, or blue and purple. Write the same color or groupings on pieces of paper at an established Finish Line (a wall or a board) for each team.
2. Have a relay race. Each team will use a felt pen corresponding to their team's color.
3. The first person from each team will walk or run from the Start to the Finish Line.
4. At the Finish Line, that person will write the name of a food (his or her team's color) that keeps us healthy.
5. Then return to the team and pass the writing implement to the next team member.

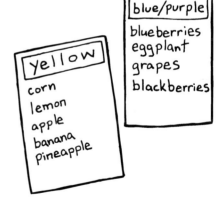

Fitness Fun *(cont.)*

Kick and Score!

1. Divide the class into relay teams.
2. Fill empty milk cartons with bits of crumpled paper to create "balls." Each student should have one ball.
3. Mark "goals" at the end of the play area. You might draw chalk squares or use large boxes with the openings on the side.
4. Each "team" of students will line up behind one another. The first student in each line will kick a "ball" to the other end, try to score, and run back to the team. **Note:** Once the runner kicks the ball to the goal he or she runs back, whether he or she has scored or not. (The "ball" stays where it was kicked.)
5. The player runs back and tags the next student in line. That player, kicking a ball toward the goal, tries to score and then returns.
6. Play continues until all teammates have run, tried to score, run back, and sat down.

Practice Balancing

- Place a line of tape on the floor. Have students place one foot in front of the other to walk on the tape.
- Have students try balancing on one leg and then the other.
- Shift to a starting position for running a race. Notice how hands and feet are used to balance.
- Ask students to balance on one hand and one foot. Challenge them to do it for 30 seconds.

Let's Make Bread

Have students act out the process of wheat being made into bread. (Think *Little Red Hen*.)

1. Sway and wave your arms like wheat in the field.
2. Imagine you are cutting wheat using a scythe. Try a chopping motion.
3. Grind the wheat to make flour. Clasp hands together, stretch arms out, and make large circular movements.
4. Stir wheat and other ingredients. Pretend to hold a bowl with one hand and stir with the other. Then switch hands for stirring and holding.
5. Knead bread dough with hands. Squeeze the dough at least 10 times.
6. Place bread in the oven, close the door, then open the door and take the bread out of the oven. Mmm....

Baseball

Talk about baseball with students. Explain that baseball is a team sport. It is an outside sport. People on the baseball team do different things. Discuss the "jobs" each player has:

- The **pitcher** throws the ball.

- The **batter** tries to hit the ball with a bat. Batters who hit the ball get to run around the bases. If they get all the way around, a home run is scored!

- The **catcher** catches the ball if the batter misses. The catcher throws the ball back to the pitcher.

- Players in the outfield try to catch the ball if the ball is hit.

1. Share the picture. Discuss the actions people use when they play baseball. What muscles do they use? Who needs strong legs? Who needs strong arms? Who needs good eyes?

2. Try these actions together. Inside, practice the throwing, catching and batting motions used to play baseball or use a crumpled paper ball and a ruler to practice with classmates. Run in place by desks to practice running to base.

3. What other baseball actions can you practice?

4. If possible, practice outside using equipment. Take turns practicing skills for each position, or play a real game!

Swimming

Swimming can be an outdoor or an indoor sport. When people swim, they use different motions to move through the water. These movements are called "strokes."

1. Look at the pictures. What parts of your body do you use to swim?
2. Copy what the swimmer is doing with his or her arms in each stroke.
3. Sit on the floor and try to kick. Keep your legs straight!

freestyle—This is also called the "crawl" stroke.

breaststroke—Swimmers kick their legs like a frog to do this stroke. Their arms and legs stay under water. Only their shoulders and heads pop out of the water.

butterfly—Swimmers raise both arms at once so they look like butterfly wings.

backstroke—Swimmers lie on their backs, move their arms, and kick their legs.

Staying Active

Weather changes. Sometimes it is cold and sometimes warm. But we can always find ways to stay active. Going for a walk is a type of exercise, and so is playing soccer.

1. What sport or activity do you like to do in warm weather?

   _____

2. What sport or activity do you like to do in the cold weather?

   _____

3. Draw a picture of your favorite kind of exercise.

4. Which muscles do you use to do your favorite kind of exercise?

   arms   **legs**   **back**   **shoulders**   **all**

Fitness Challenge

Teacher Directions: Explain to students that a challenge is something that requires effort. Many physical activities are challenging. We can practice, and our skills will improve.

1. Introduce a different challenge every day. Have students log their results in their journals on the "Fitness Challenge Log" page.

2. Measure *how far* or *how fast* students can go, or *how many* repetitions students can do in a specific amount of time.

3. Have students keep track using their journals.

Challenge Suggestions

1. Mark off a distance in the playground and have students do different movement activities. Try skipping, running, hopping on one foot, or sliding sideways.

2. As they improve, make the distance longer or have them increase laps going back and forth. Or, see how far they can go in a certain amount of time.

3. Count how many jumping jacks, sit-ups, push-ups, or squats students can do in 30 seconds. How about in one minute?

4.	Do you have a sand or grass area? If so, introduce the standing broad jump. How far can students jump?	5.	Add some balancing activities on "inside" days. Can students stand on one foot for 30 seconds? Can they do it holding one leg out in front or behind them?

Food and Fitness
JOURNAL

This journal belongs to:

My Personal Health Goals

Directions: Write at least one personal health goal you would like to try each week. Check each week and see how you're doing at meeting your goal.

	Met	Not Yet
WEEK _____ My personal goal this week is to _____ _____		
WEEK _____ My personal goal this week is to _____ _____		
WEEK _____ My personal goal this week is to _____ _____		
WEEK _____ My personal goal this week is to _____ _____		
WEEK _____ My personal goal this week is to _____ _____		
WEEK _____ My personal goal this week is to _____ _____		

My Exercise Log

Directions: Place a *tally mark* in the box each time you do the exercise.

1. Touch toes.	2. Wiggle.	3. Hop on one foot.
4. Run in place.	5. Jumping jacks.	6. Do arm circles.
7. March in place.	8. Climb a mountain.	9. Do squats.
10. Do desk pushups.	11. Do chair squats.	12. Jump rope.
13. Bicycle.	14. Dance.	15. Do small arm circles.
16. Do leg raises.	17. Sway.	18. Bend and squat.
19. Do neck rolls.	20. Do shoulder scrunches.	21. Do tiptoe stretches.
22. Lean sideways.	23. Lean forward and back.	24. Hula hoop.

My Healthy Meal

This is a healthy meal. I have added foods from every group.

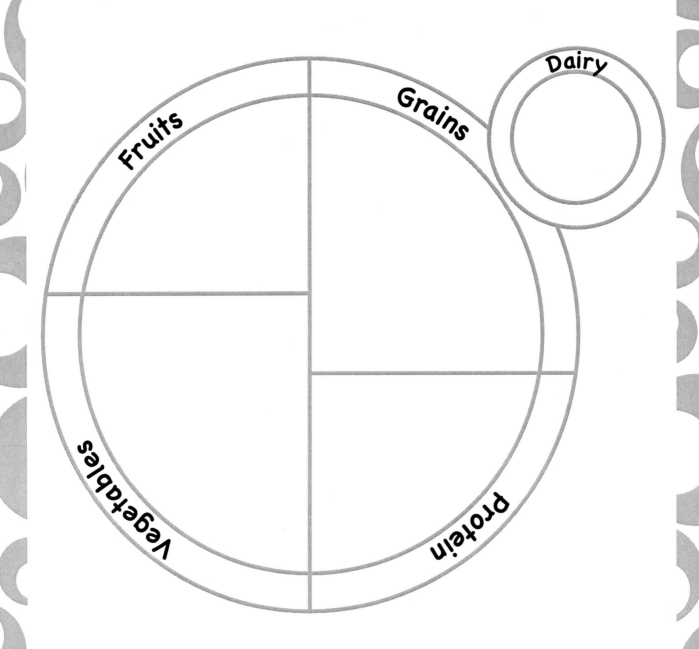

Teacher Note: The outline above is based on the USDA My Plate graphic. See page 5 for more information on this informative USDA site.

My Most Important Foods

I have learned about the five food groups. The most important thing I

learned is _____ .

Here is information and a drawing of a food I eat from each group.

Fruit: _____ It is good for me because _____ .	
Vegetable: _____ It is good for me because _____ .	
Protein: _____ It is good for me because _____ .	
Dairy product: _____ It is good for me because _____ .	
Grain product: _____ It is good for me because _____ .	

Healthy Foods to Try

Every food group has a long list of foods. Some foods are new to me.
Here are foods from each food group that I would like to try.

Fruits	Dairy

Vegetables

Protein	Grain

Being Healthy

Being healthy is important. When you are healthy you can do many things.

Here is a picture of me. I am _____

To be healthy you need to:

1. _____

2. _____

Being Safe

There are many ways to take care of myself and to be safe. Here are some things I do to take care of myself.

1. _____

_____

_____

2. _____

_____

_____

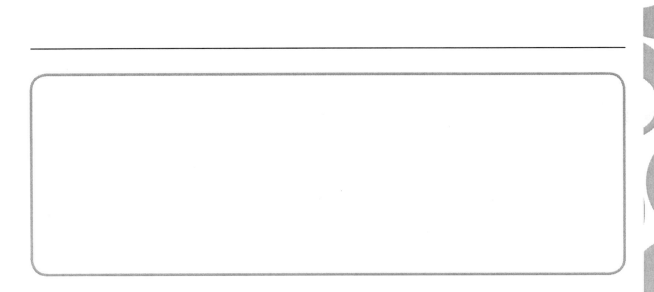

Fitness Challenge Log

Student Name _____

Age _____

Challenge	Date	Distance	Time

Journal

_____

_____

_____

_____

_____

_____

_____

_____

_____

Journal

_____

_____

_____

_____

_____

_____

_____

_____

_____

_____

_____

_____

_____

_____

Answer Key

pages 14–15 (Fruits Checklist 1 & 2)
Answers will vary.

page 16 (What Is a Fruit?)
Answers will vary.

page 17 (Fruits That Grow on Trees)
Apple 12 seeds
Orange 16 seeds
Pear 14 seeds
Check tracing.

page 18 (Fruits That Grow on Vines)
1 & 2. Check tracing and coloring.
3. pumpkin

page 19 (Citrus Fruits)
1 & 2. Check tracing and coloring.
4. Vitamin C

page 20 (A Rising Star)

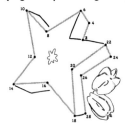

page 21 (Favorite Fruits)
1. bananas, apples
2. 1
3. 2
4. Answers will vary.

page 22 (Which Juice Is Our Favorite?)
1. Check student tally marks for understanding.
2–4. Answers will vary.

pages 23–24 (Vegetables Checklist 1 & 2)
Answers will vary.

page 25 (Vegetables)
1–5. Check student markings (circles) for understanding.

page 26 (Our Favorite Vegetables)
1. corn
2. peas
3. carrots
4. Answers will vary.

page 27 (Green Vegetables)
1. spinach   kale
    broccoli   Brussels sprouts
    peas   asparagus
2. We eat the leaves of kale and spinach.
3. Answers will vary.

page 28 (Hidden Green Beans)
2. 10 green beans; check coloring

page 29 (Peppers)
Each pepper should be colored according to the code.

page 30 (Colorful Vegetables)
Possible answers:
   red: beets, cabbage, lettuce, pepper, tomato
   orange: carrots, pepper, sweet potato
   yellow: corn, pepper
   green: asparagus, broccoli, cabbage, celery, green beans, green pepper, kale, lettuce, peas, spinach
   blue: none
   purple: eggplant
   white: cauliflower, corn, potato
1. blue; purple
2. green

page 31 (Whole Grains Checklist)
Answers will vary.

page 32 (Whole Grains)
Label suggestions:
1. grain growing in field
2. grain harvested or cut with combine
3. grain stored in silos
4. grain ground into flour

page 33 (Whole Wheat Tic-Tac-Toe)
All the pictures should be colored except the egg, the smoothie, and the baked potato.

page 34 (Oats)

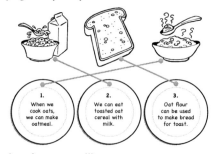

4. Answers will vary.

page 35 (Corn)

6—muffins, corn bread, cereal, pancakes, tortillas, and popcorn

page 36 (Whole Grain Foods)

1. rye bread
2. corn tortilla
3. oat cereal
4. popcorn
5. wheat crackers
6. beef barley soup

page 37 (Dairy Foods Checklist)
Answers will vary.

page 38 (Dairy Foods)

1. milk
2. cheese
3. yogurt
4. cottage cheese
5. ice cream
6. pudding

Ice cream and pudding should be circled.

page 39 (Where Milk Comes From)
No answer key necessary.

page 40 (Say Cheese)
Answers will vary. Check tally marks.

page 41 (Dairy or Not?)
Row 1—broccoli
Row 2—banana
Row 3—green beans
Row 4—hamburger

page 42 (Dairy Foods for Every Meal)
Answers will vary. Check for understanding.

page 43 (Protein Foods Checklist)
Answers will vary.

page 44 (Protein Foods)
No answer key necessary.

page 45 (Animals Give Us Protein)

Answers will vary.

page 46 (Legumes)
Possible answers:

1. bean sprouts, garbanzo beans, peas
2. chickpeas (garbanzo beans)
3. peas, peanuts
4. lentils, dry beans
5. peanuts

page 47 (Peanuts Are Legumes)
1. Check the colors used.
2. 7 peanuts

page 48 (Nuts We Eat)
1. Answers will vary.
2. Answers will vary.
3. Check explanations.

page 49 (Tree Nuts)
1. 3 walnuts
3. 6 almonds

page 50 (Nutrition Is Important)
1. Check that a food from each food group is listed.
2. Check that student illustrations are appropriate for each food group.

page 51 (Sometimes Foods)
1. Answers will vary.
2. Answers will vary.
3. Answers will vary.

page 52 (Riddle Time)
1. pumpkin, tomato
2. carrot, peanuts
3. almonds, walnuts
4. fish, shrimp
5. grapes, watermelon
6. wheat bread, brown rice

page 53 (Making Good Food Choices)
Check responses and discuss choices.

page 54 (Find the Healthy Foods)

m	s	a	e	p	b	m	h	y	l
t	e	h	r	c	u	a	e	o	d
h	k	s	a	f	n	k	s	g	m
r	a	p	t	y	r	o	l	u	a
i	c	l	j	u	i	c	e	r	k
c	n	o	o	t	a	t	o	p	t	c
w	a	t	e	r	m	e	l	o	n
z	p	l	t	g	s	p	u	k	u
a	f	p	e	a	c	h	m	b	t
e	s	e	e	h	c	r	a	o	s

3. Answers will vary.
4. Answers will vary.

page 55 (Hidden Message)

```
        C  H  E  E  S  E
        P  E  A  S
        A  P  P  L  E
        L  E  T  T  U  C  E
     O  A  T  M  E  A  L
  P  E  A  C  H
T  U  R  K  E  Y
```

Mystery Word: healthy

page 56 (Keeping Our Food Safe)
Possible answers:
1. Wash fruits and vegetables.
2. Keep refrigerated foods cold.
3. Wash dishes.
4. Wash your hands.

Answer Key *(cont.)*

page 57 (Things We Do to Stay Healthy)
1. brush teeth
2. exercise
3. drink water
4. eat breakfast
5. sleep
6. wash hands

page 58 (Wash Your Hands)
1. Correct sequence:
   child looking at dirty hands
   child turning on water
   child soaping hands
   child washing hands
   child rinsing hands
   child drying hands
2. Answers will vary.

page 59 (Take Care of Yourself)
1. getting rest and drinking water
2. Cross out these pictures of children spreading germs:
   children sharing a drink (left)
   child rubbing eyes (right)
   child coughing into hands (left)

page 60 (Healthy Teeth)
1. Answers will vary.
2. toothbrush, toothpaste, and floss should be circled.
3. Answers will vary. Check for understanding.
4. Answers will vary.

page 61 (Inside a Tooth)
1–3. Check colors.
4. crown
5. pulp, dentin

page 62 (Sleep Is Good for Us)
1. Answers will vary.
2. Answers will vary. Check the clock for accuracy.
3. Answers will vary. Check the clock for accuracy.

page 63 (Stay Safe)

page 64 (Stranger Danger)
All questions and answers should be discussed to clarify answers and situations.
1. smiley face (yes)
2. no smiley face (no)
3. smiley face (yes)
4. smiley face (yes)
5. no smiley face (no)

page 65 (Bones Need Calcium)
1–3. Answers will vary but check for understanding.

page 66 (Being Active)
1. Possible answers are suggested but consider others as well:
   run, stomp, walk, swing, jump, slide, hop, skip, climb, kick a ball, catch a ball, throw a ball
2. Check for reasonable art.

page 67 (Did You Stretch Today?)
Monitor students to make certain they are stretching correctly and not bouncing.

page 68 (Daily Movements)
1. making a bed—bend, stretch, pull
2. sweeping the floor—pull, walk, sway, push
3. taking out the trash—lift, walk, carry
4. picking up toys—bend, carry, lift, reach
5. watering plants—walk, carry, balance
6. clearing the table—walk, carry, balance, stretch

page 69 (Playing with Movement)
1–5. Observe and discuss each group's presentation.

page 70 (Animal Moves)
Accept realistic alternative responses.
1. crawl; slither
2. swim
3. dig
4. run; leap
5. slither
6. hop; run
7. climb; swing
8. reach
9. flap
10. leap

pages 71–79
No answer key necessary.

page 80 (Swimming)
1. Accept reasonable answers such as: We use our arms and legs to swim.

page 81 (Staying Active)
Answers will vary.

page 82 (Fitness Challenge)
Check the student charts at the end of the week.